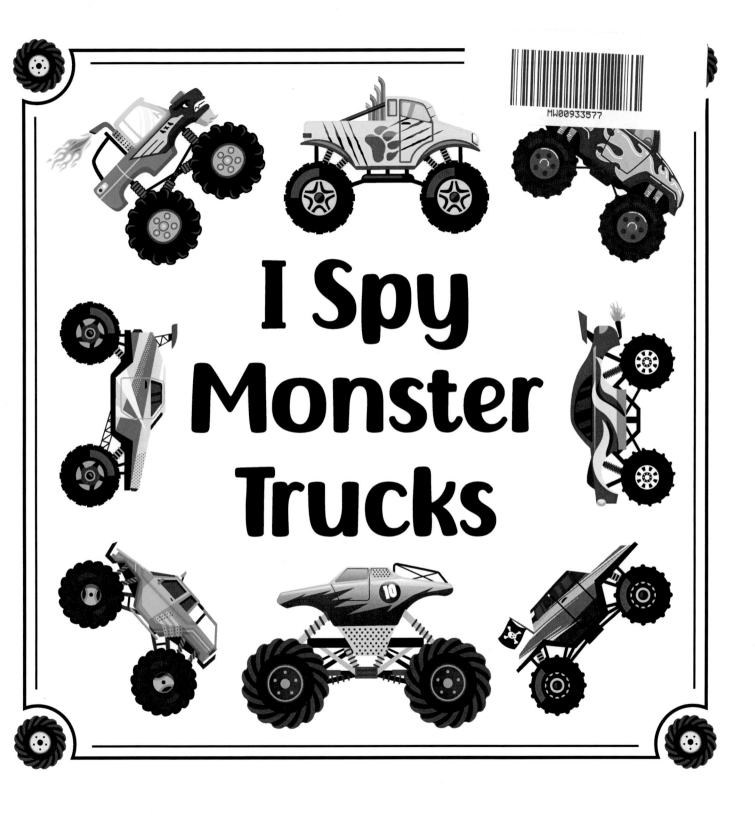

I Spy Monster Trucks

This Book Belongs To:

_____

_____

This Activity Book is for Vehicles Lovers! Each beautiful page will keep your little kid entertained for hours.

I Spy with my little eyes, all the monster trucks like this one! →

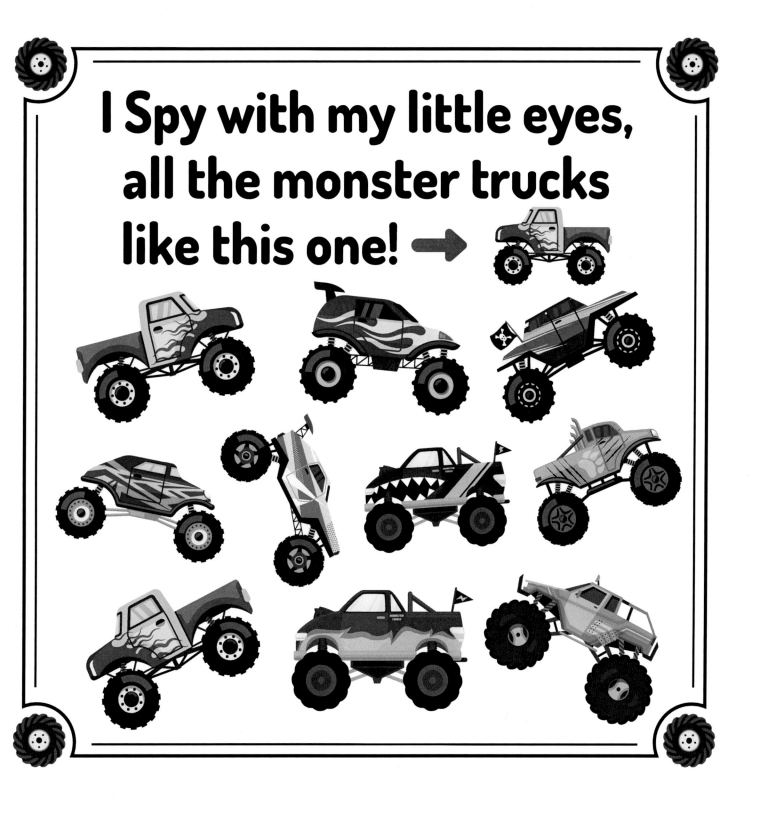

Congrats!
You guessed correctly

There were 2 of them
in the picture

I Spy with my little eyes, all the monster trucks like this one! →

Congrats!
You guessed correctly

There were 3 of them in the picture

I Spy with my little eyes, all purple monster trucks!
Can you find them all?

Congrats!
You guessed correctly

There were 5 of them
in the picture

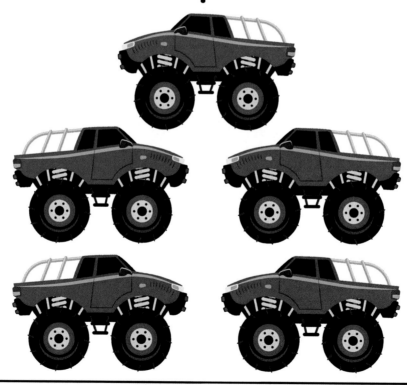

I Spy with my little eyes, all the ice cream trucks like this one! →

Congrats!
You guessed correctly

There were 4 of them in the picture

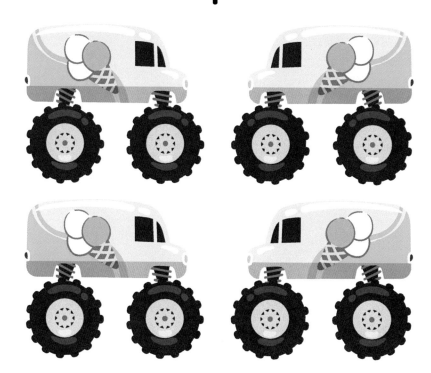

Find 3 of the same monster trucks

Congrats!
You guessed correctly

Here are 3 of the same monster trucks in the picture

I Spy with my little eyes, all the monster trucks like this one! →

Congrats!
You guessed correctly

There were 2 of them in the picture

I Spy with my little eyes, all green monster trucks!
Can you find them all?

Congrats!
You guessed correctly

There were 4 of them
in the picture

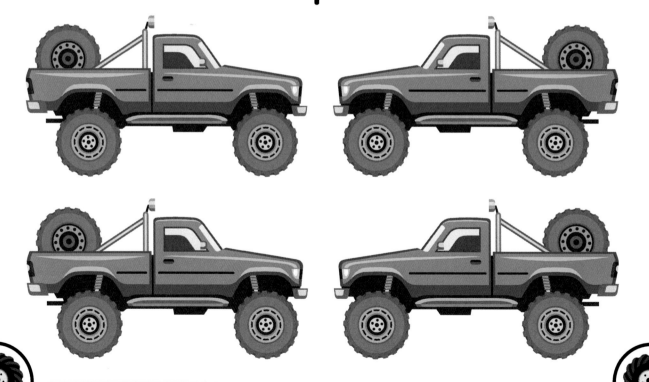

I Spy with my little eyes, all the monster trucks like this one! →

Congrats!
You guessed correctly

There were 3 of them
in the picture

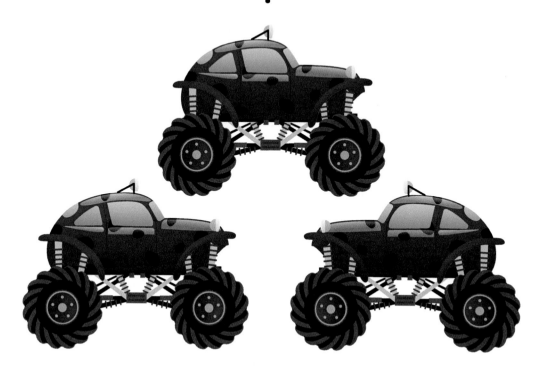

I Spy with my little eyes, all the school bus trucks like this one! →

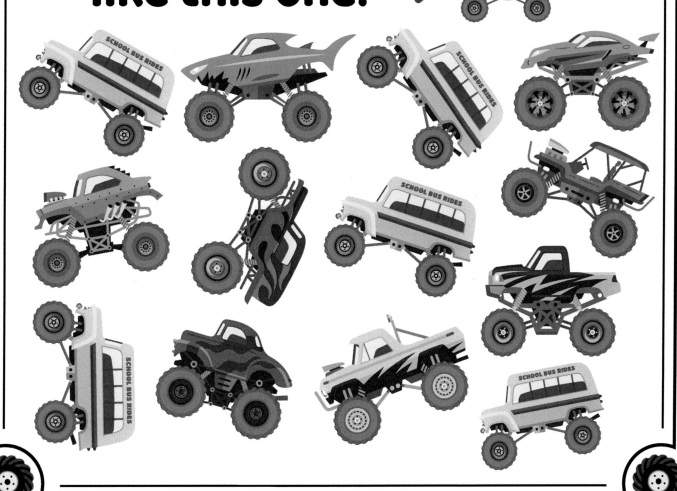

Congrats!
You guessed correctly

There were 5 of them
in the picture

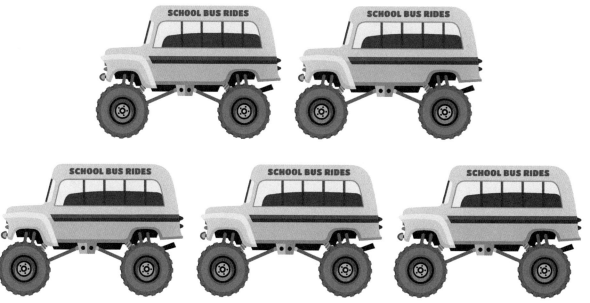

Find 3 of the same monster trucks

Congrats!
You guessed correctly

Here are 3 of the same monster trucks in the picture

I Spy with my little eyes, all the monster trucks like this one! →

Congrats!
You guessed correctly

There were 4 of them
in the picture

I Spy with my little eyes, all the monster trucks like this one! →

Congrats!
You guessed correctly

There were 2 of them
in the picture

I Spy with my little eyes, all the police trucks!
Can you find them all?

Congrats!
You guessed correctly

There were 4 of them
in the picture

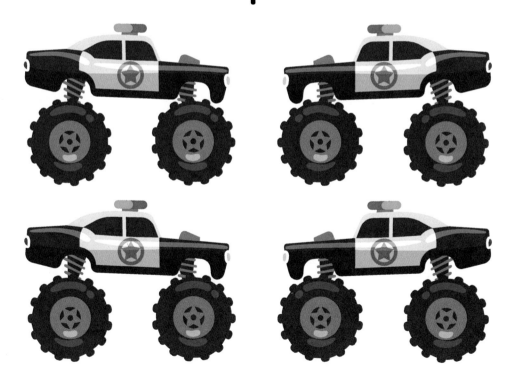

I Spy with my little eyes, all the monster trucks like this one! ➡

Congrats!
You guessed correctly

There were 3 of them in the picture

I Spy with my little eyes, all yellow monster trucks!
Can you find them all?

Congrats!
You guessed correctly

There were 2 of them
in the picture

Find 2 of the same
monster trucks

Congrats!
You guessed correctly

Here are 2 of the same monster trucks in the picture

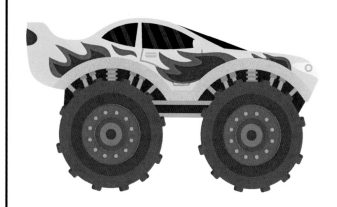

I Spy with my little eyes, all the monster trucks which has the American flag!

Congrats!
You guessed correctly

There were 6 of them
in the picture

I Spy with my little eyes, all the monster trucks like this one! →

Congrats!
You guessed correctly

There were 7 of them
in the picture

I Spy with my little eyes, all the pirate-flagged trucks!
Can you find them all?

Congrats!
You guessed correctly

There were 3 of them in the picture

I Spy with my little eyes, all the monster trucks like this one! →

Congrats!
You guessed correctly

There were 4 of them
in the picture

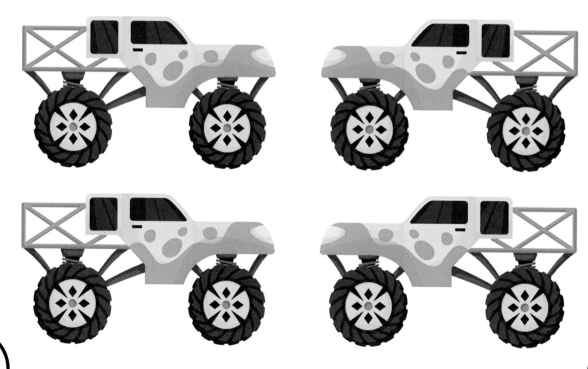

Your feedback is invaluable to us!

It helps us create better books for your child.

We genuinely hope you enjoyed our products,

and we'd greatly appreciate your

thoughts and suggestions.

Thank you for being a part of our journey

to inspire young minds!

Also check our beautiful books in our store

Kerri R. Scholastic

Made in United States
Orlando, FL
22 December 2024

56442054R00024